DEMONS IN THE DARKNESS

LessonsForLifeBooks.com

Unless otherwise indicated, any and all Scripture quotations or references contained in the Cross Man Comics are taken from the Holy Bible, King James version. All Rights Reserved.

IMPRINT A Cross Man Comics Adventure

Demons in the
Darkness 3

© 2016 by
Keith M. Hammond
is published by
Lessons for Life Books, Inc.
St. Paul, MN 55116

ISBN 13: 978-1938588822. Printed in the U.S.A.

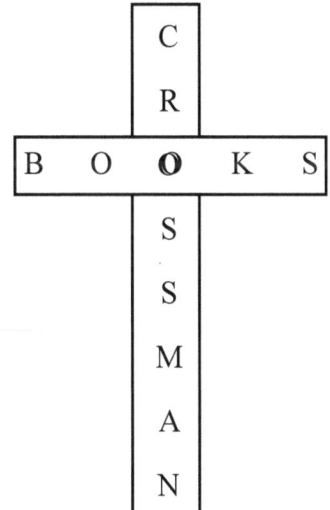

```
        C
        R
B   O   O   K   S
        S
        S
        M
        A
        N
```

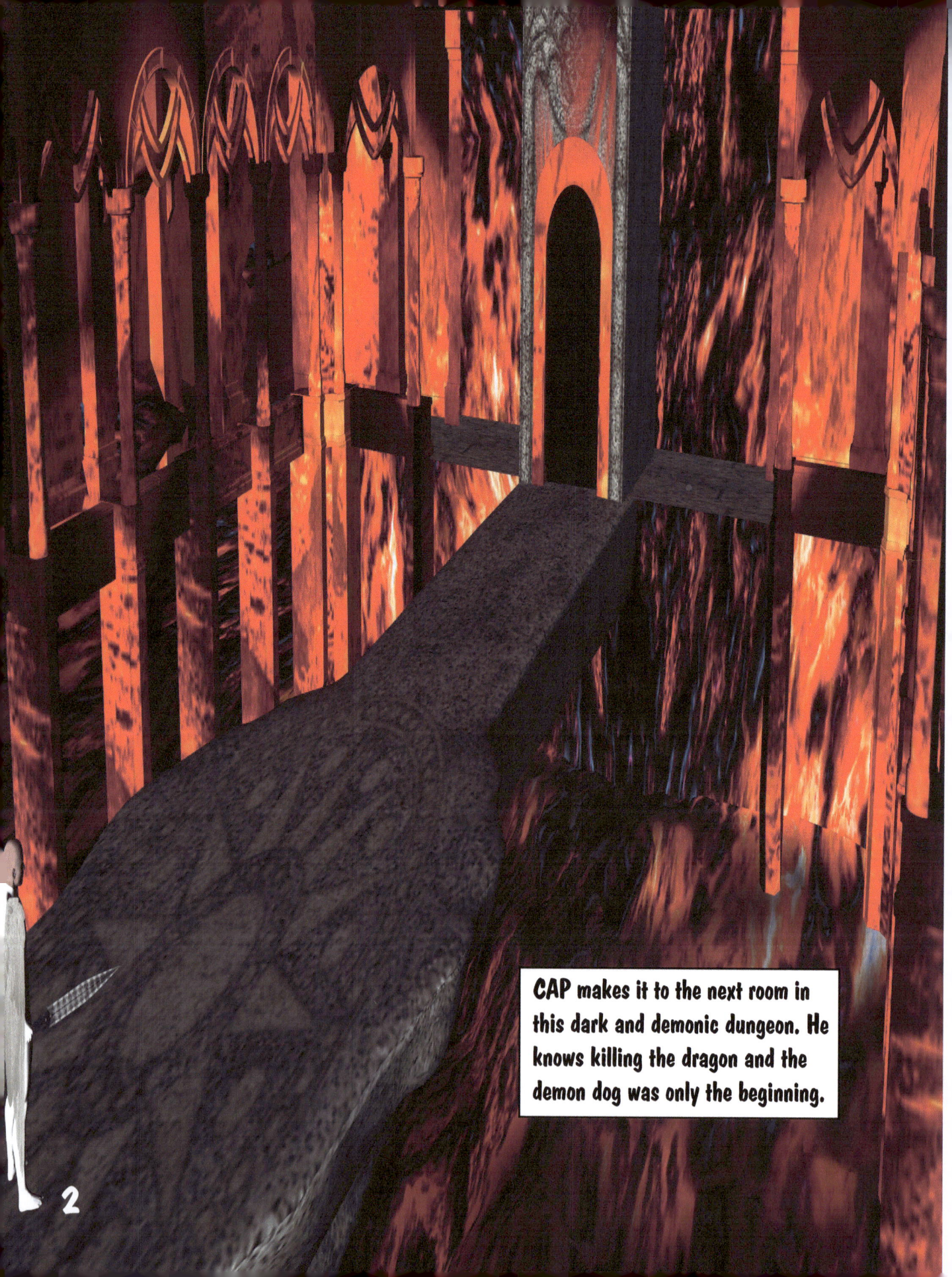

CAP makes it to the next room in this dark and demonic dungeon. He knows killing the dragon and the demon dog was only the beginning.

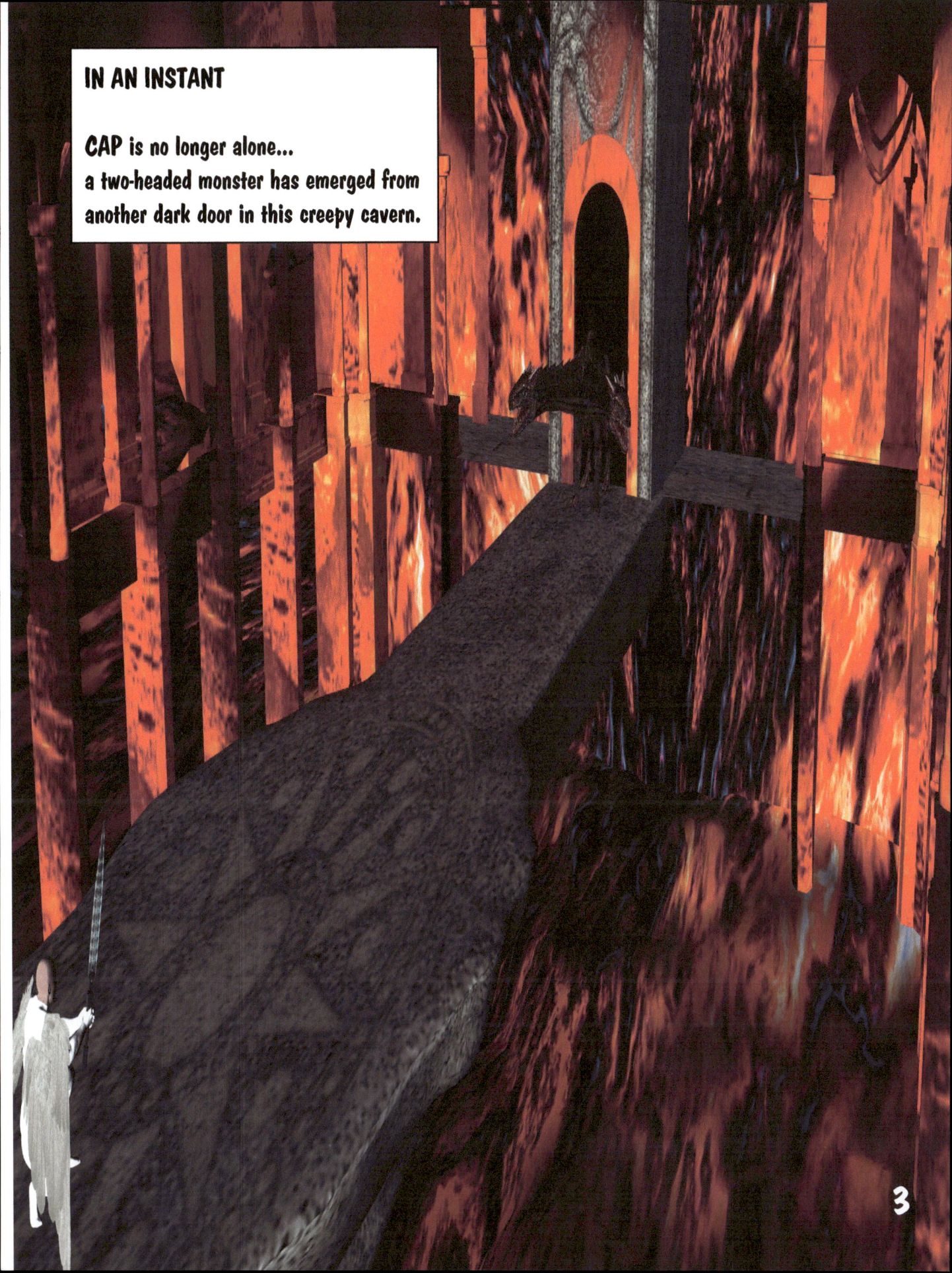

IN AN INSTANT

CAP is no longer alone...
a two-headed monster has emerged from
another dark door in this creepy cavern.

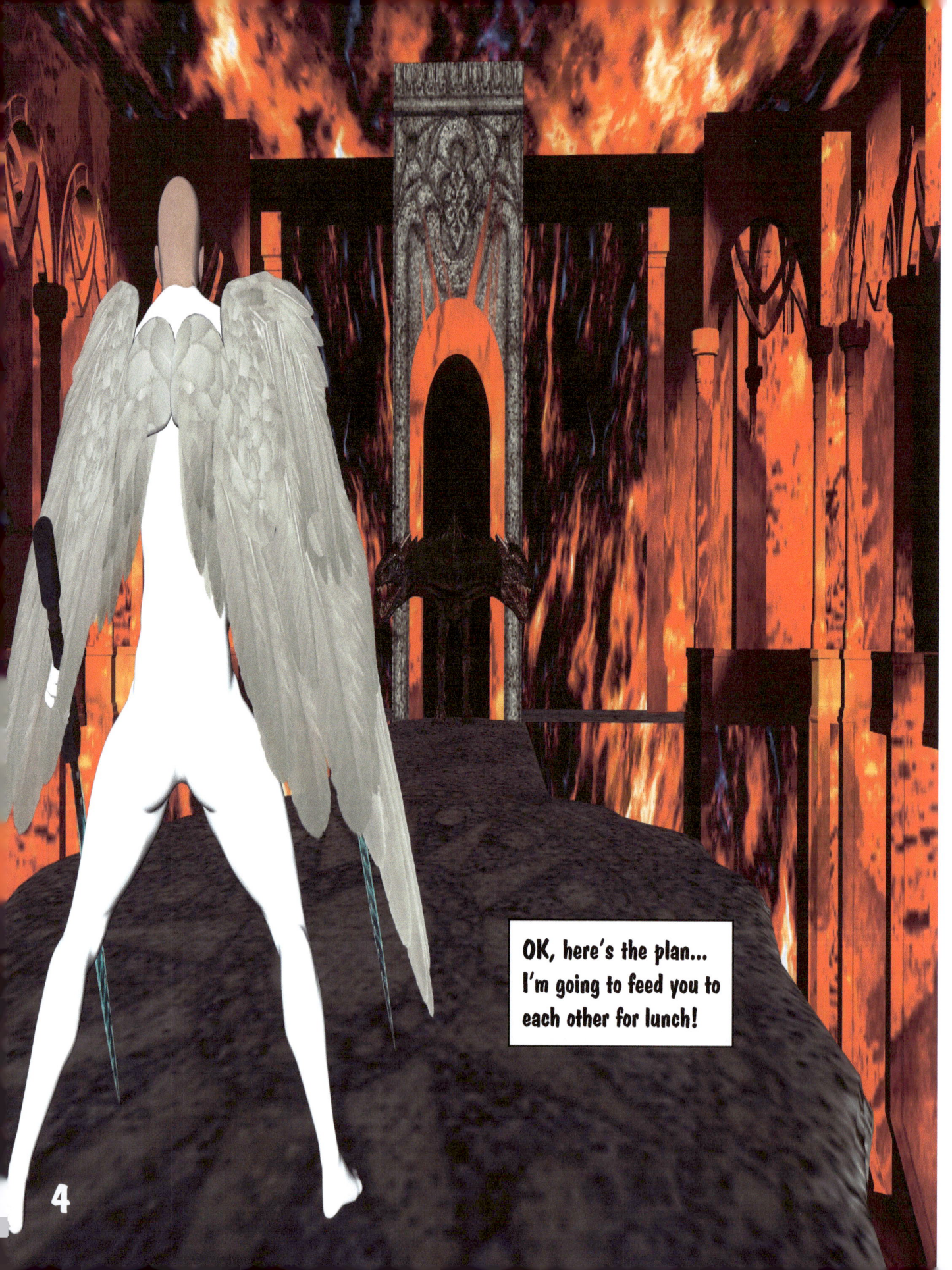

OK, here's the plan...
I'm going to feed you to
each other for lunch!

4

Before CAP could get the words out, a second two-headed creature shows up behind the first one.

CAP...it's CIRCUIT...
That space you're in is rotating.
The room behind that door is only accessible once every six minutes.

But you have to leave ASAP, **GENERAL DARKWING** is here to take over for **SARGE.**

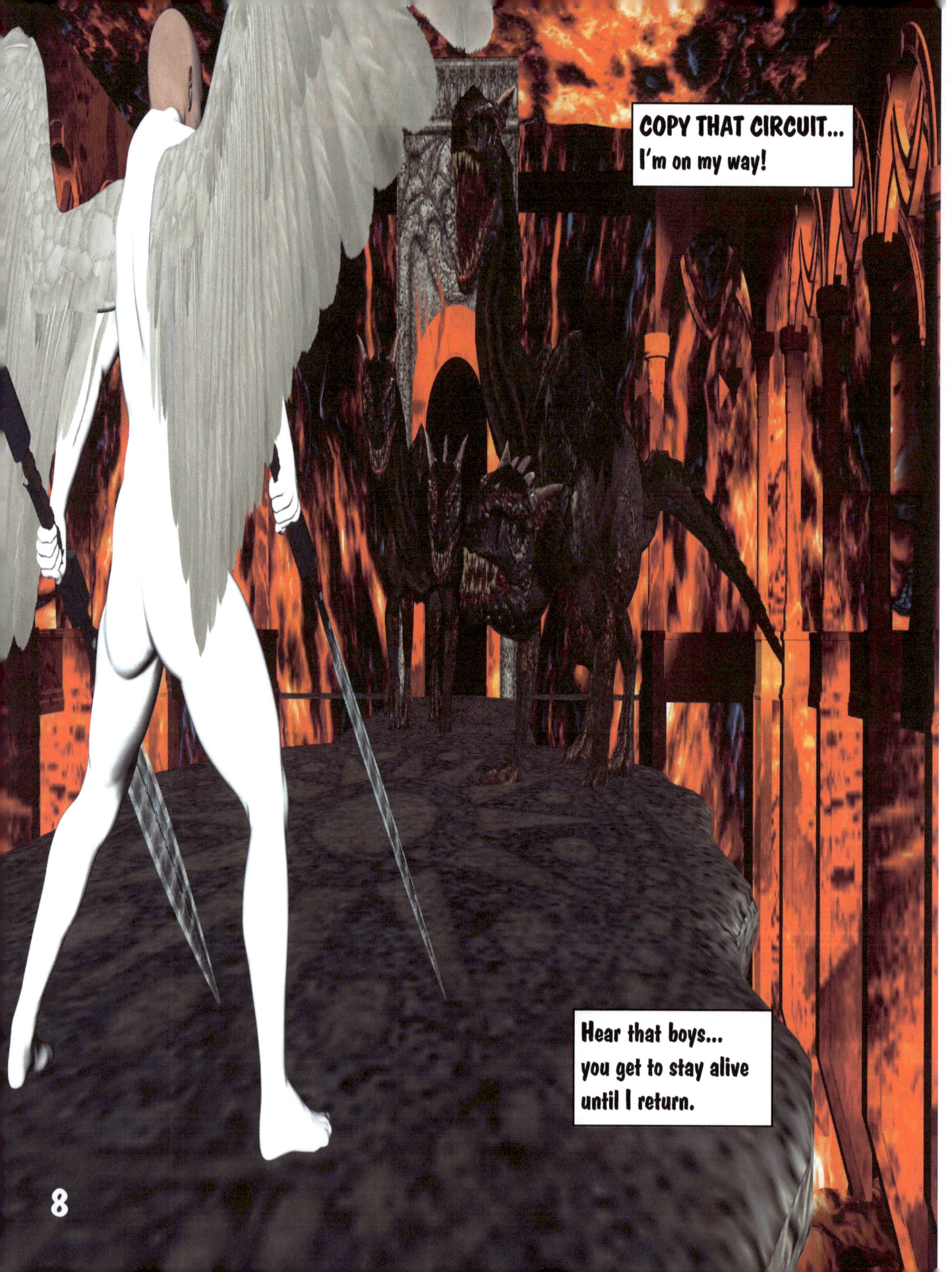

A WHILE LATER...at OPS

CAP...it's great to see you again. SARGE's deployment to establish our defenses on MARS was finally approved.

I need to give you this KEY... It is for extreme emergencies only. It unlocks a door to a project we call Lightning Bolt. It will kill everything in its path within a two-mile radius. We took it from Satan in another battle. Let's meet with your team & I'll tell you more.

TEAM...I need you to pay special attention to your surroundings in this battle and be sure to watch each other's back. Satan will use anything & anyone to distract you.

My instructions are simple: Wear your faith without fear. Represent that cross on your chest and be bold in battle. This team will have ZERO casualties in this war.

10

I've battled Satan before...the only way to win is through his sin. Maintain your patrol...and the enemy's history will lead us to victory.

WHILE ON PATROL... INTEL and FOX head toward the Dark Lair to check on the progress with the force field.

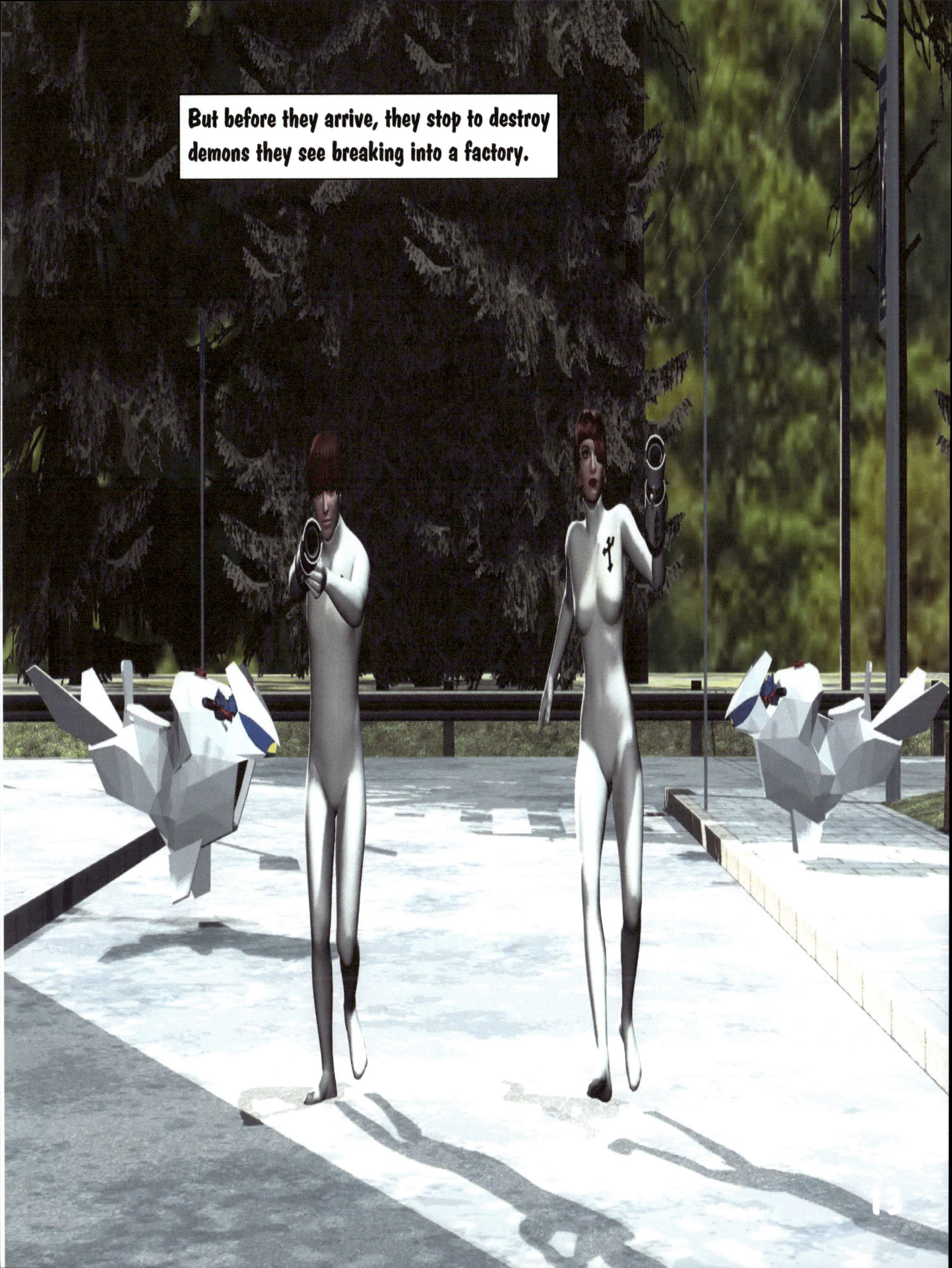

But before they arrive, they stop to destroy demons they see breaking into a factory.

WHILE ON PATROL...
Renegade and Ranger spot a problem...

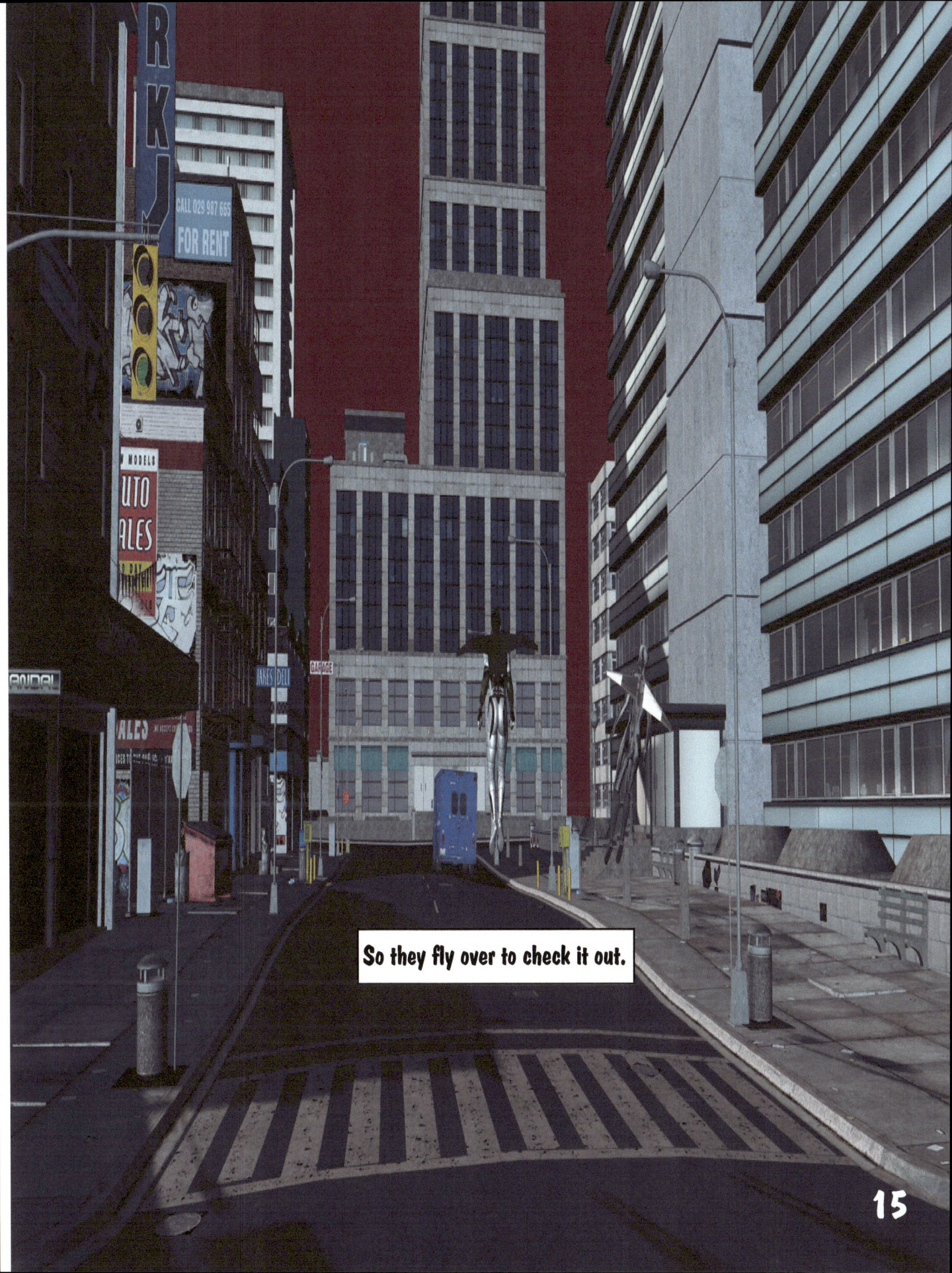

So they fly over to check it out.

WHILE ON PATROL...
Shadow stops to save kids...

...from the cancer ward of a burning hospital.

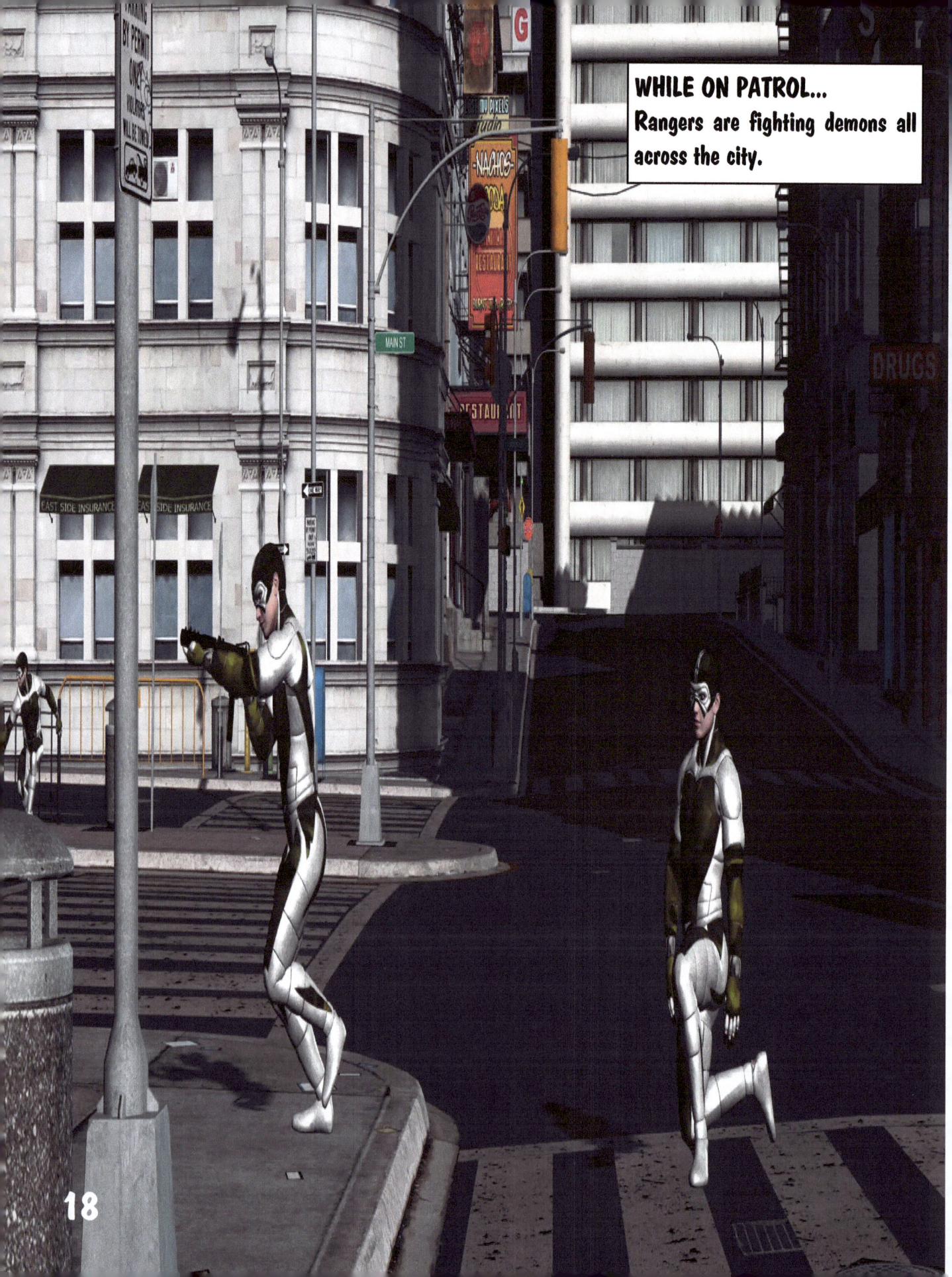

WHILE ON PATROL...
Rangers are fighting demons all across the city.

And at churches in several sectors.

19

GENERAL DARKWING
was right...

Satan uses ways to distract so his Demons can attack.
And their first target is INTEL.

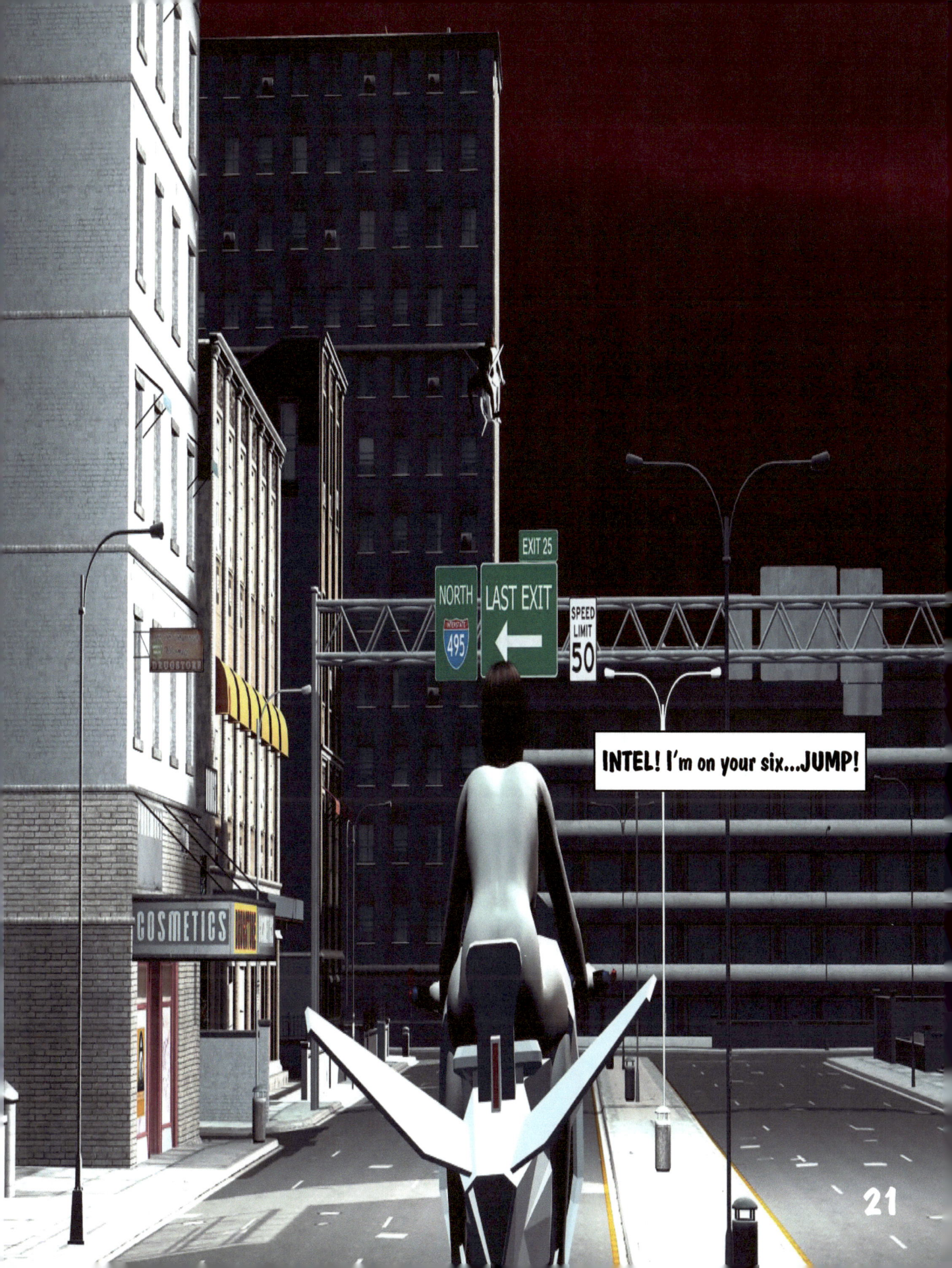

INTEL! I'm on your six...JUMP!

21

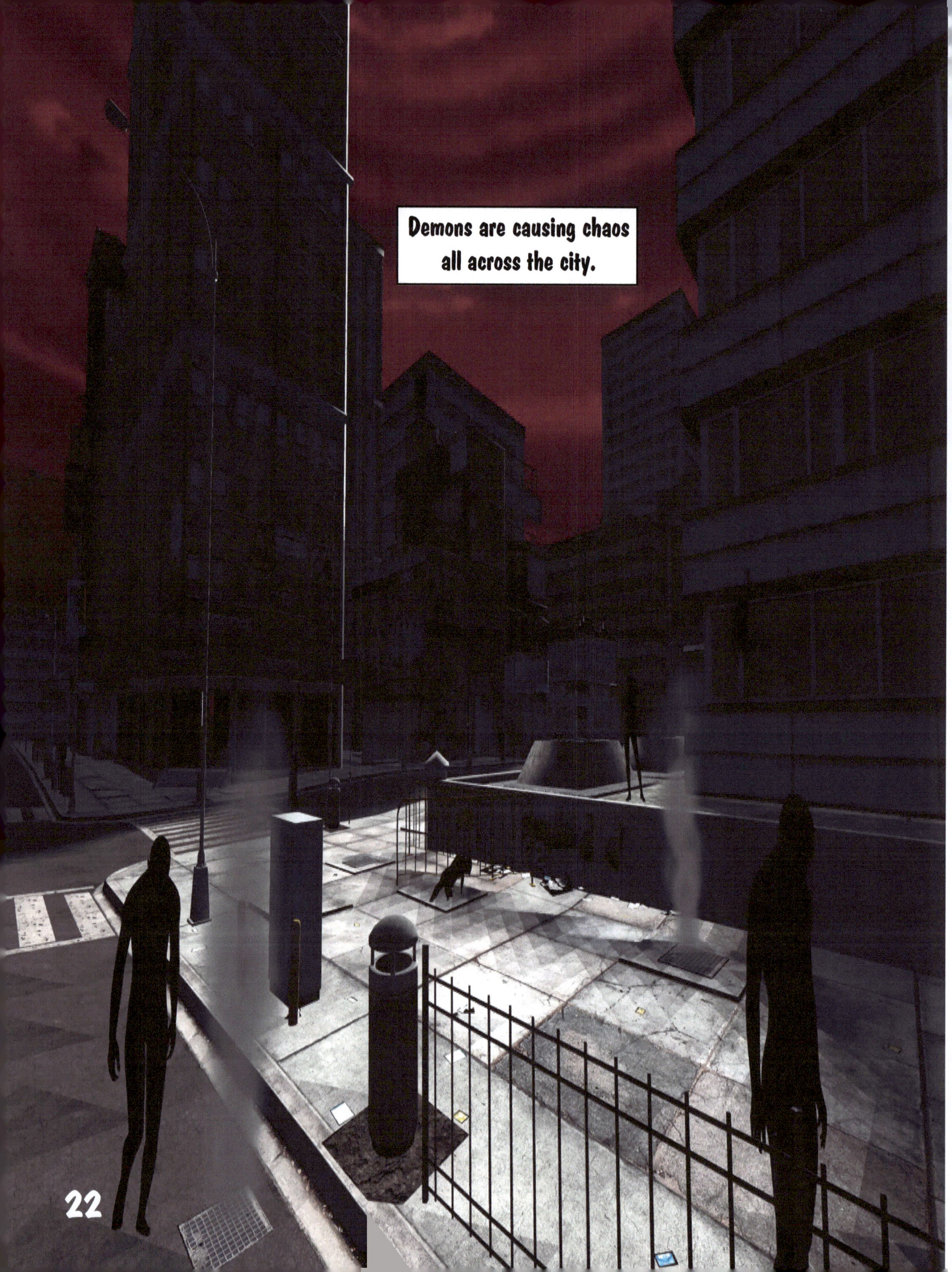
Demons are causing chaos all across the city.

People everywhere are being attacked.

23

Demons have been unleashed!

24

And no one is safe!

25

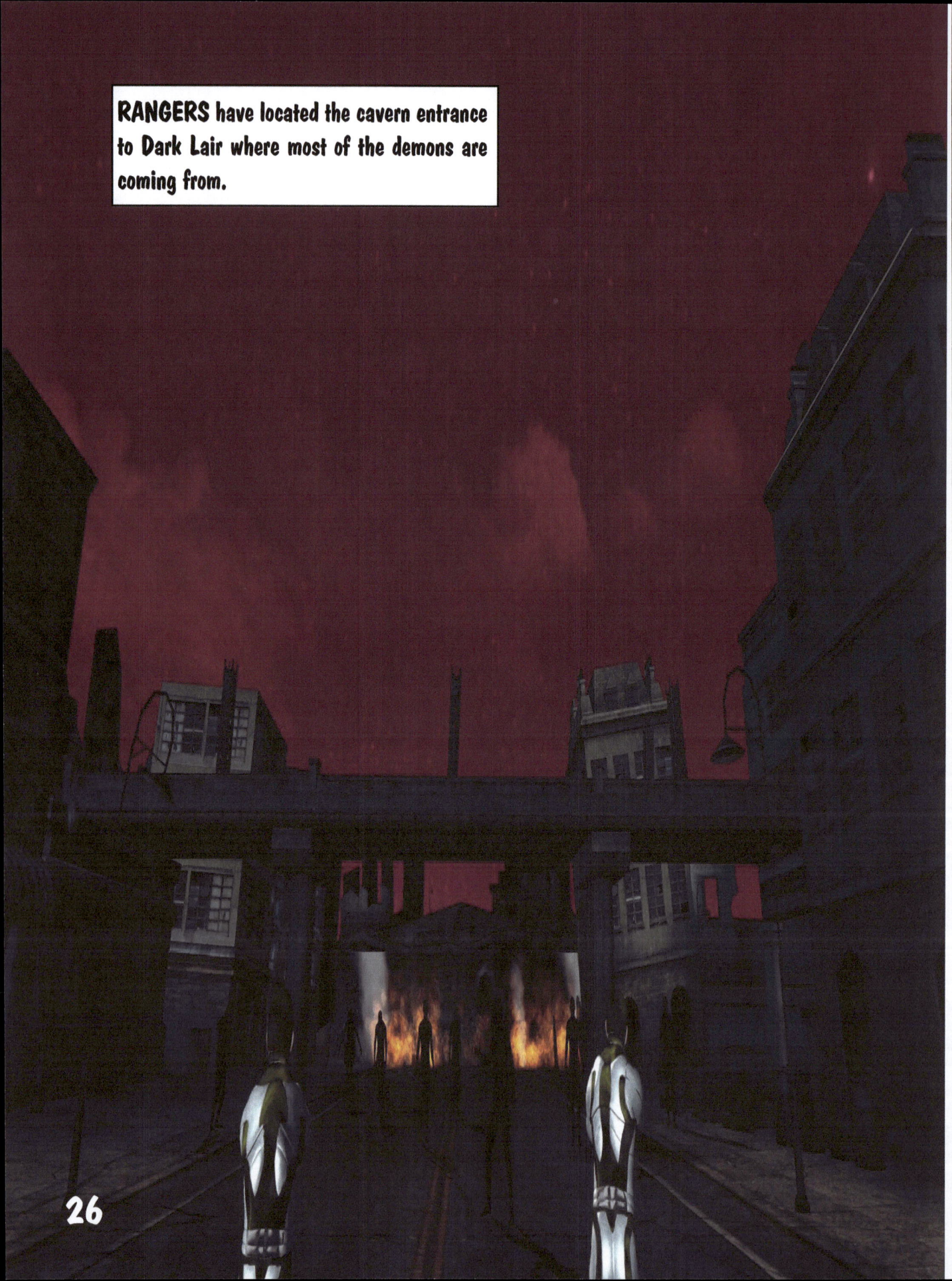

26

CAP...these are the latest images that MICRO pulled from our satellite. We need to find a way to close that cavern.

Consider it done Sir.

27

AT THE FACTORY INTEL and FOX stopped to confront demons at... INTEL is jumped.

BEFORE HE CAN REACT, he is ambushed by two demons.

INTEL fights to get out of their grasp, but the more they touch him the weaker he gets.

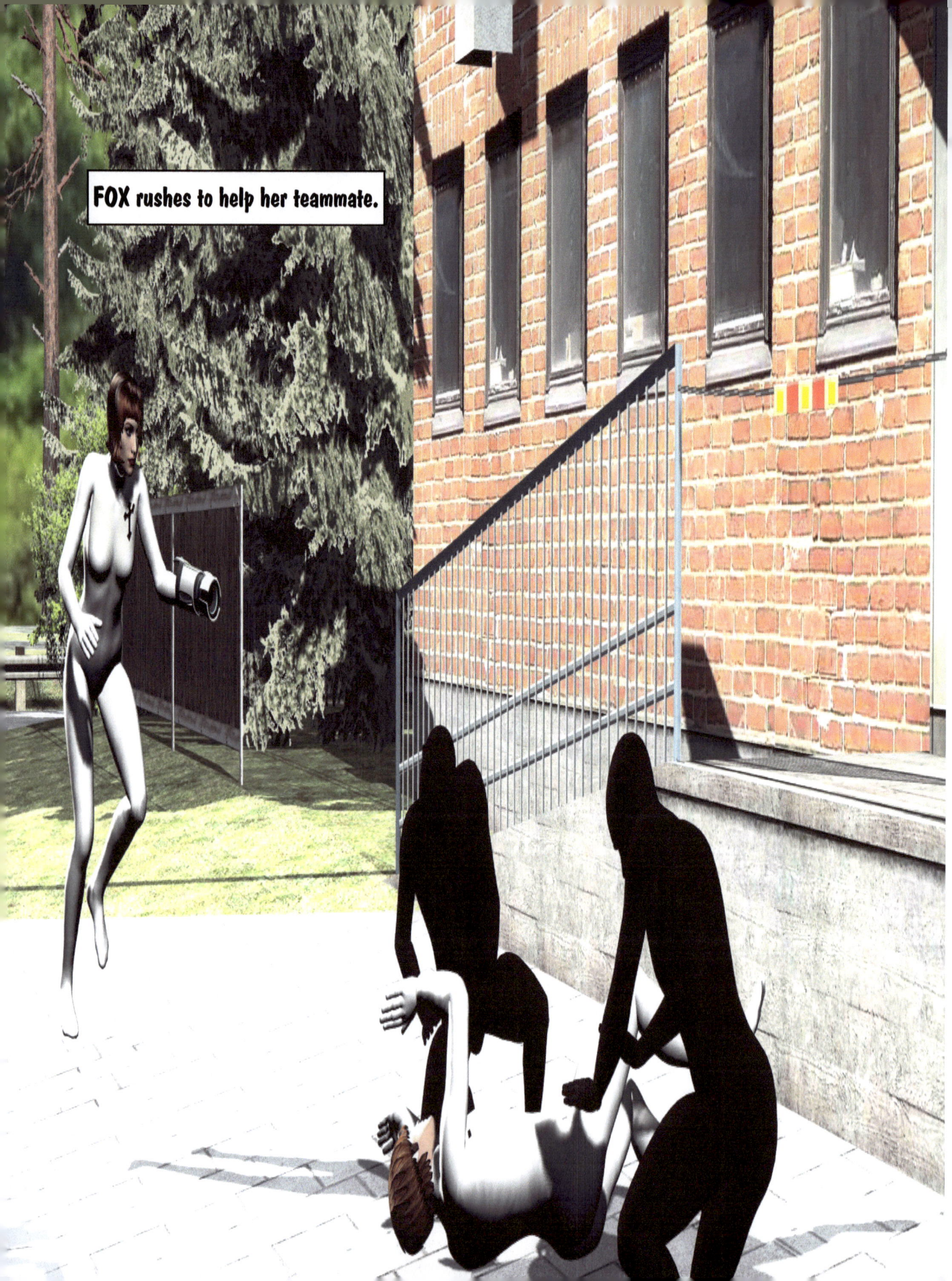

FOX rushes to help her teammate.

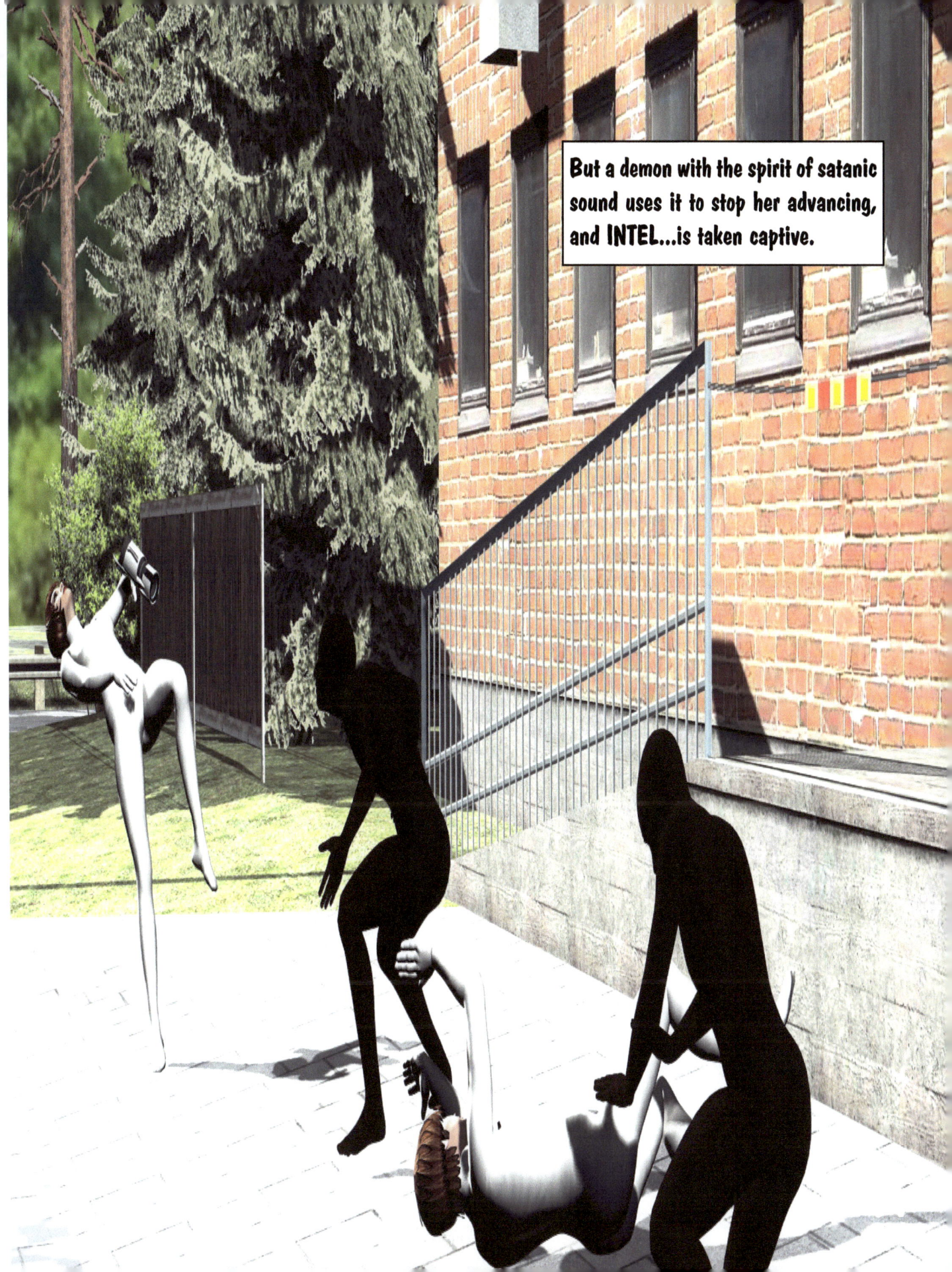

But a demon with the spirit of satanic sound uses it to stop her advancing, and INTEL...is taken captive.

INTEL has been taken hostage. INVADE Dark Lair.

With pleasure Sir.

CAP sends teams of Rangers and Soldiers to penetrate Dark Lair in search of INTEL.

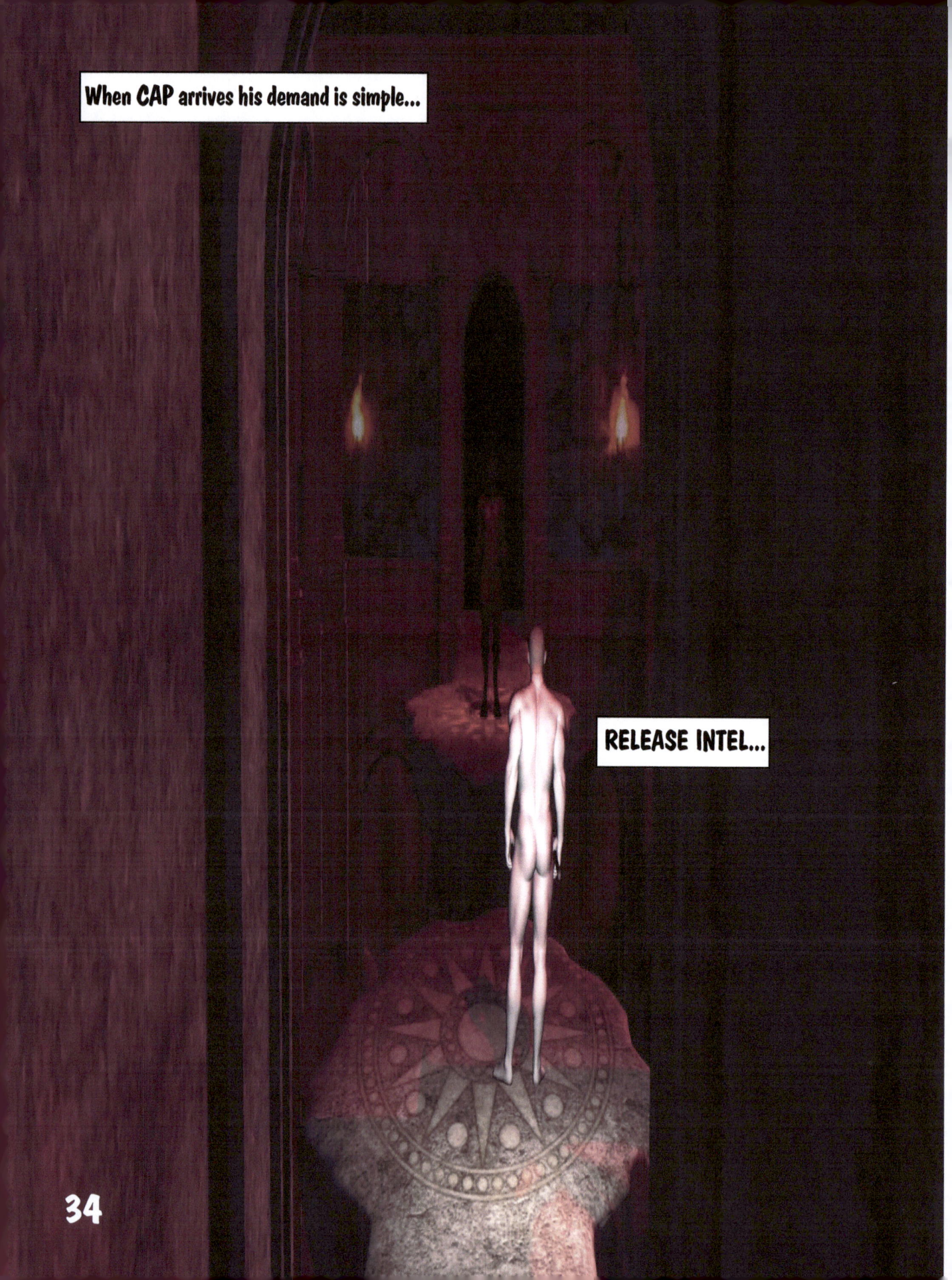

When CAP arrives his demand is simple...

RELEASE INTEL...

34

Satan responds...

Give me back the lightning bolt that was taken from me and I will release your comrade. Until then, you can deal with this dragon.

SATAN turns and walks away, leaving CAP to face another dragon...

Although reluctant to leave Dark Lair without INTEL...

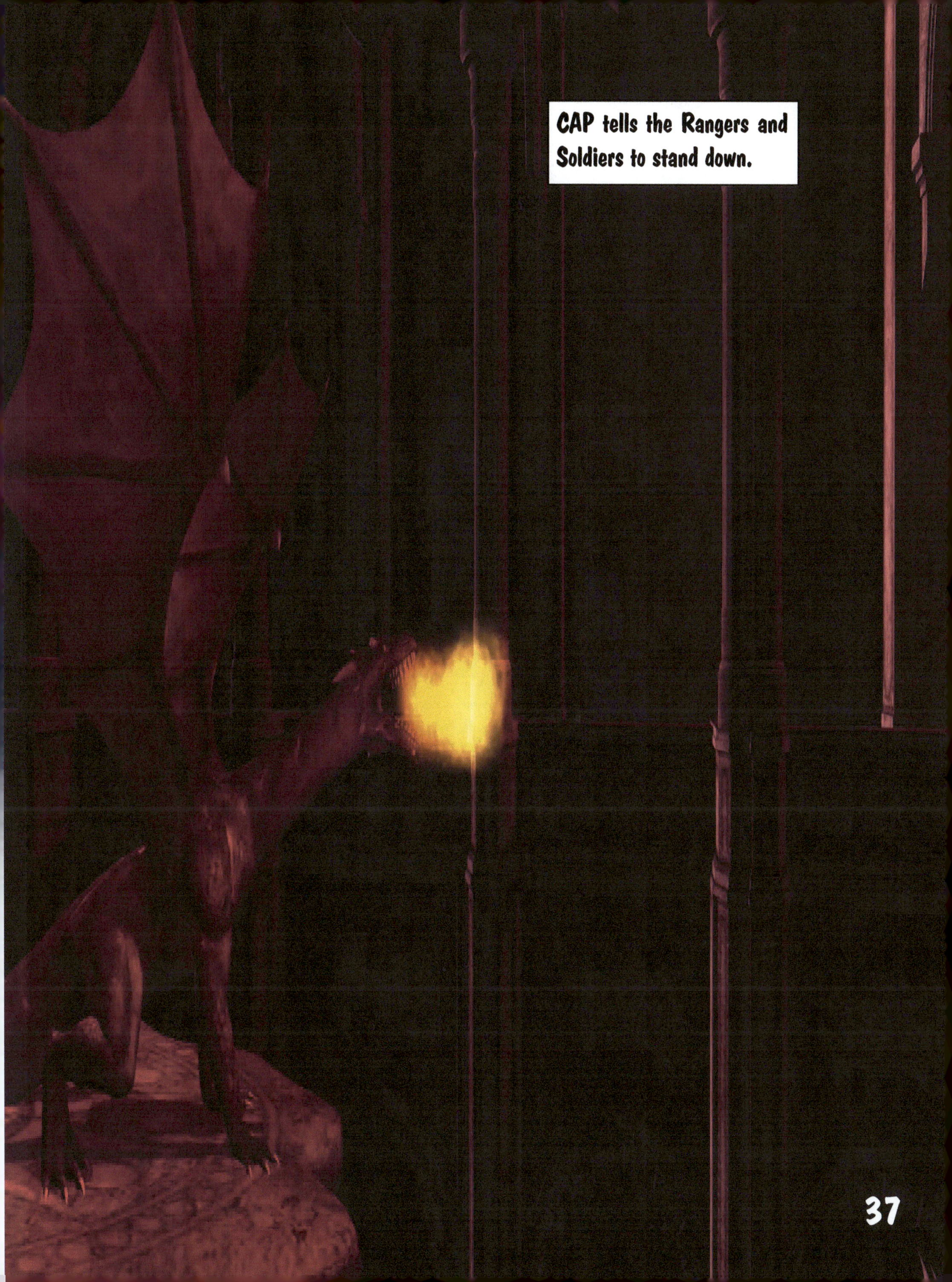
CAP tells the Rangers and Soldiers to stand down.

CAP, it's CIRCUIT...
Demons are attacking all over the city. We've given people notice on every news station to stay inside, but there may still be some at work who haven't seen it.

And CAP, the demons aren't alone. Demon Dogs and Dragons have surfaced now too.

Demons plan to take as many captive as they can in an attempt to gain some leverage to get Lightning Bolt back.

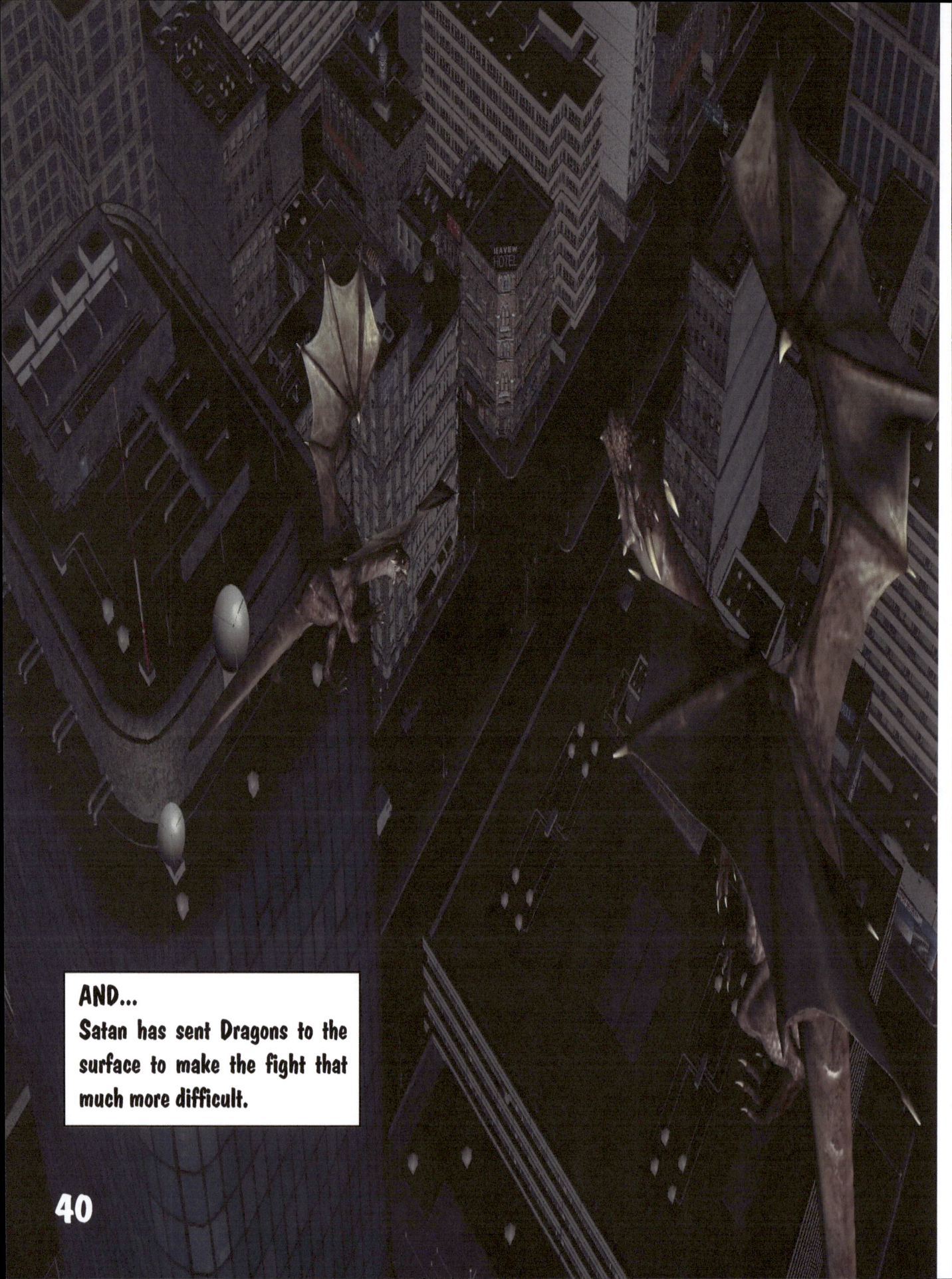

AND...
Satan has sent Dragons to the surface to make the fight that much more difficult.

So he wastes no time getting to it.

42

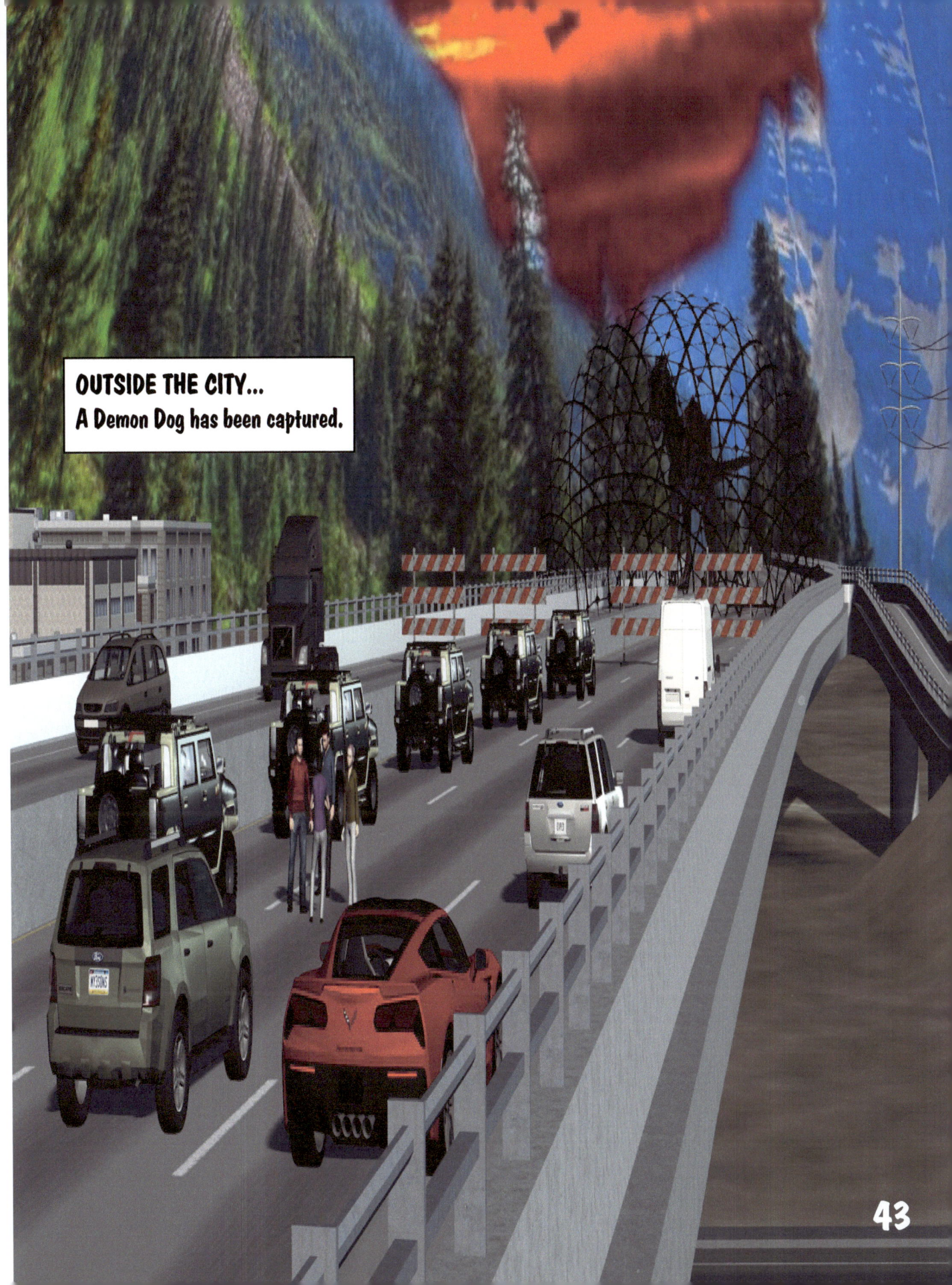

OUTSIDE THE CITY...
A Demon Dog has been captured.

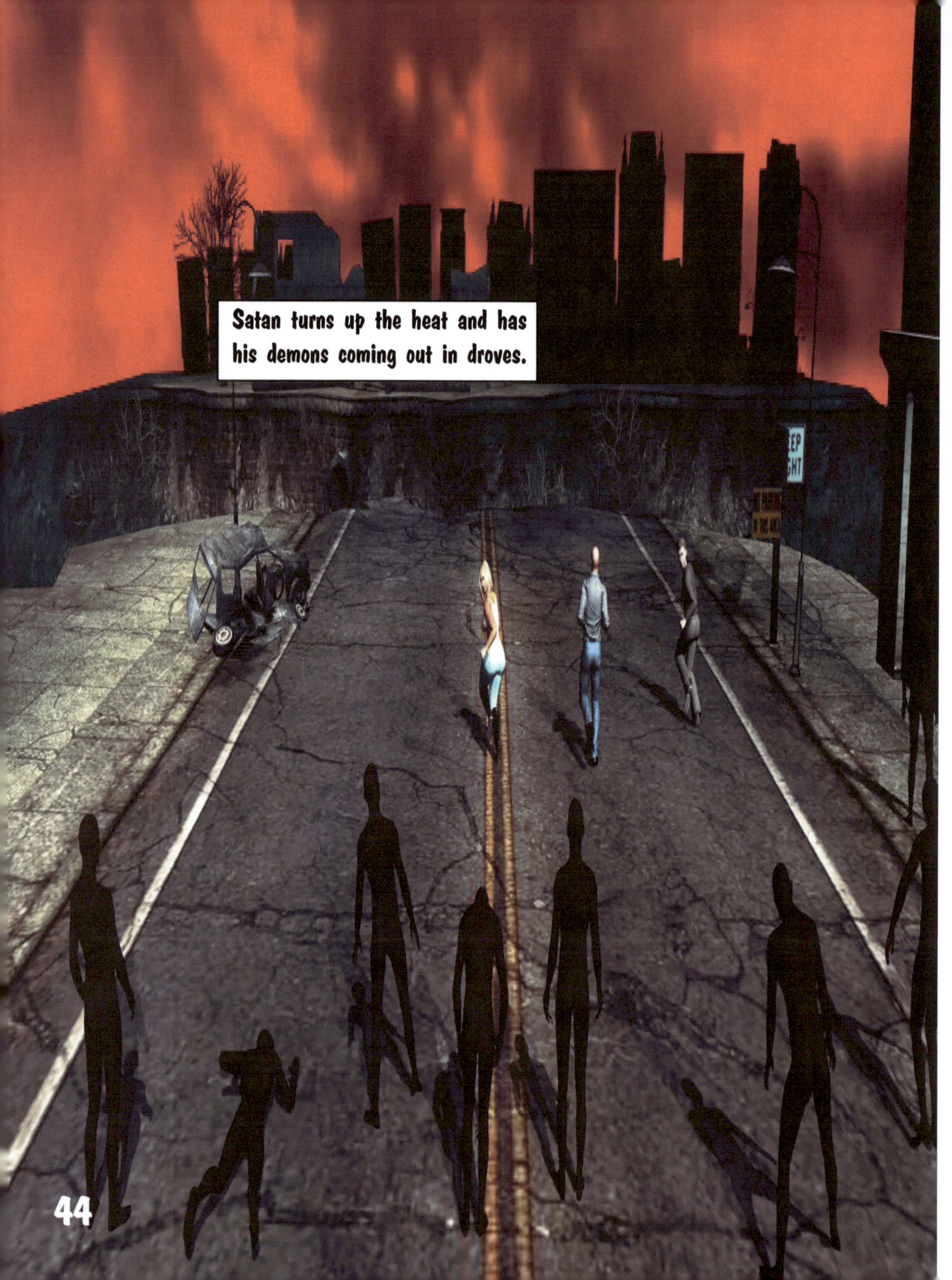

Satan turns up the heat and has his demons coming out in droves.

And people trying to get away are finding themselves trapped.

Satan erupts another explosion and dispatches even more demons.

The latest explosion makes the cavern split open twice as wide. If this continues, the cavern will eventually surround the city.

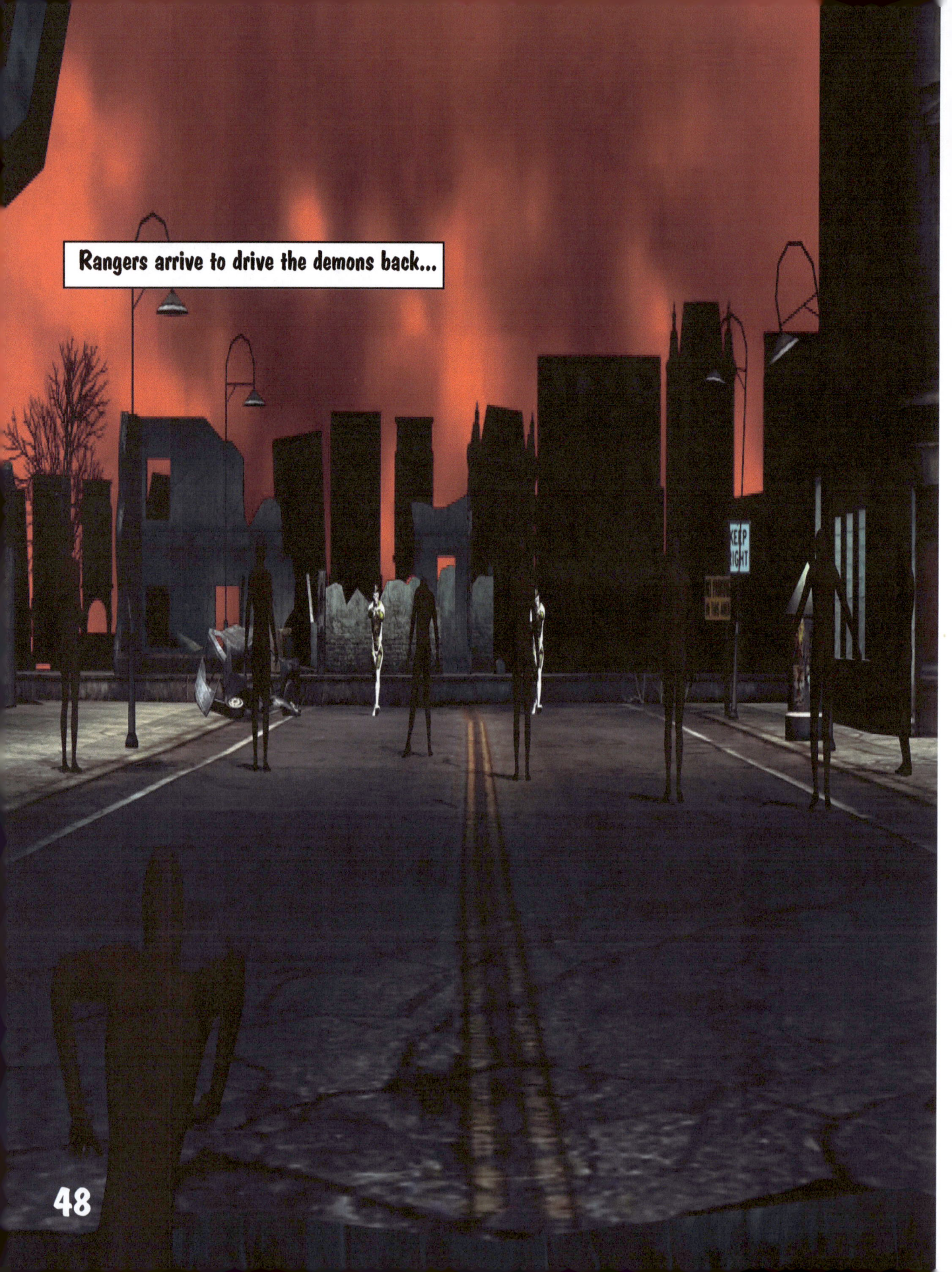

Rangers arrive to drive the demons back...

And to destroy as many as they can.

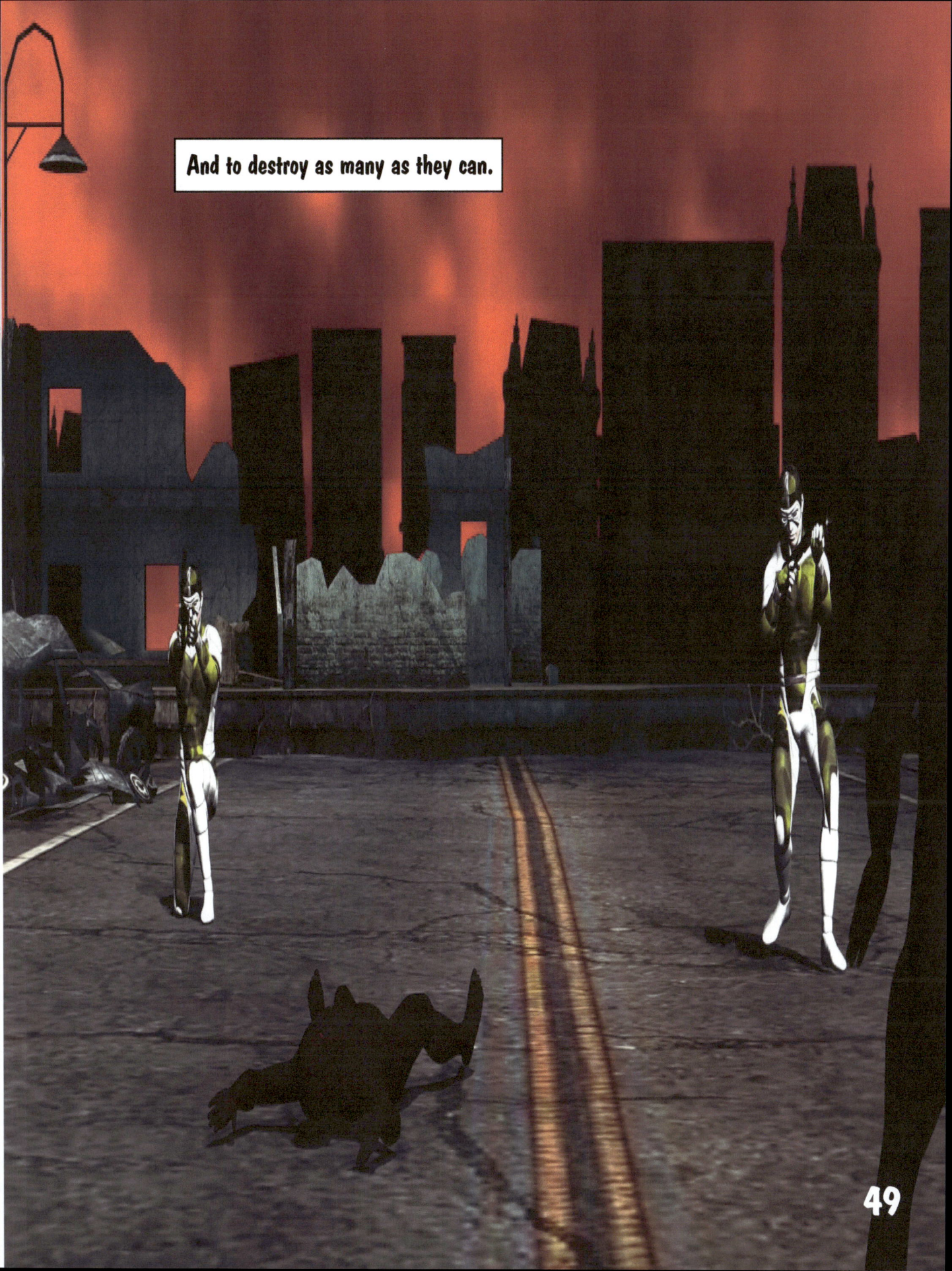

49

But demons are everywhere in the city now. RENEGADE and her Ranger team members fight to destroy them all...

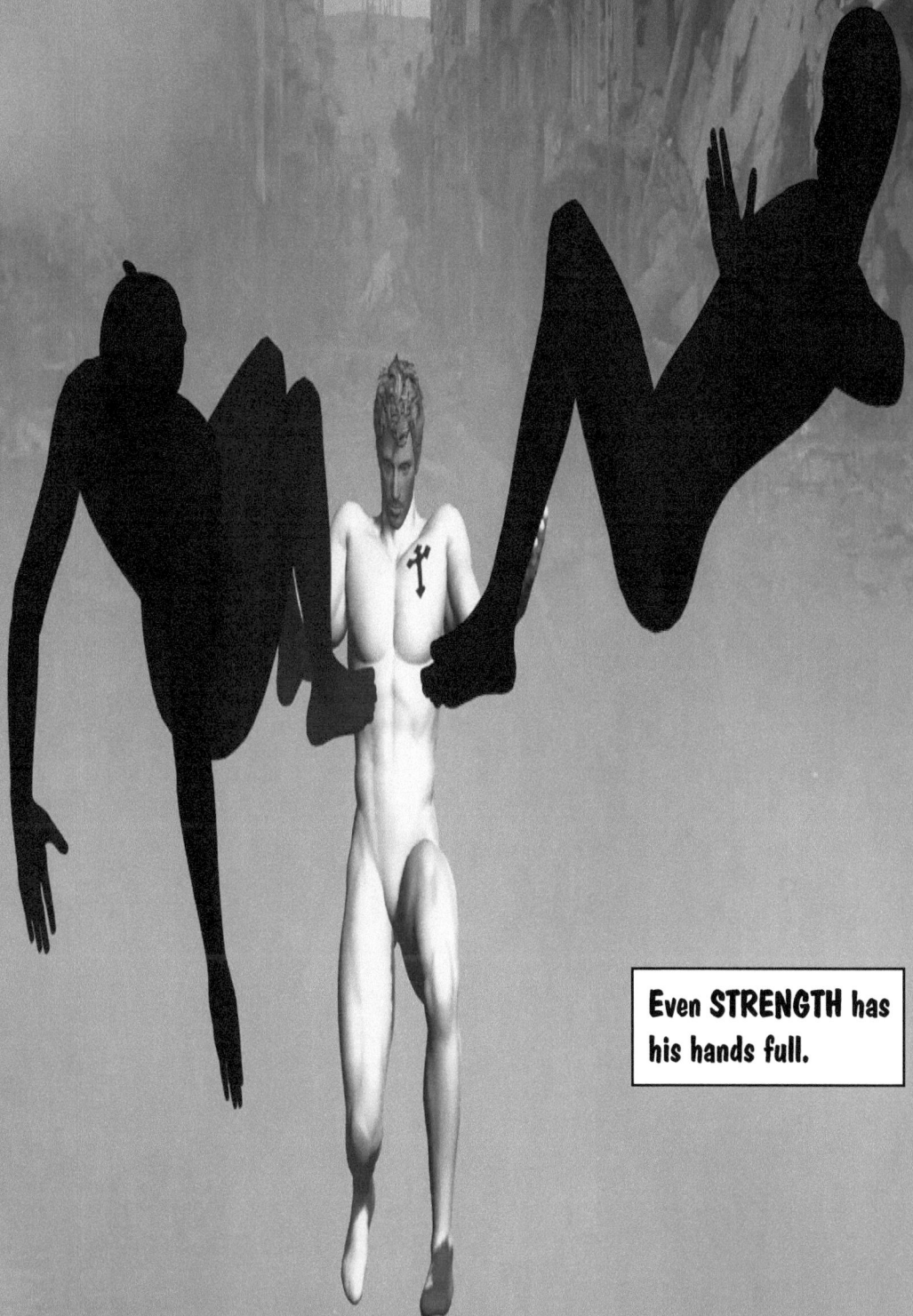

Even STRENGTH has his hands full.

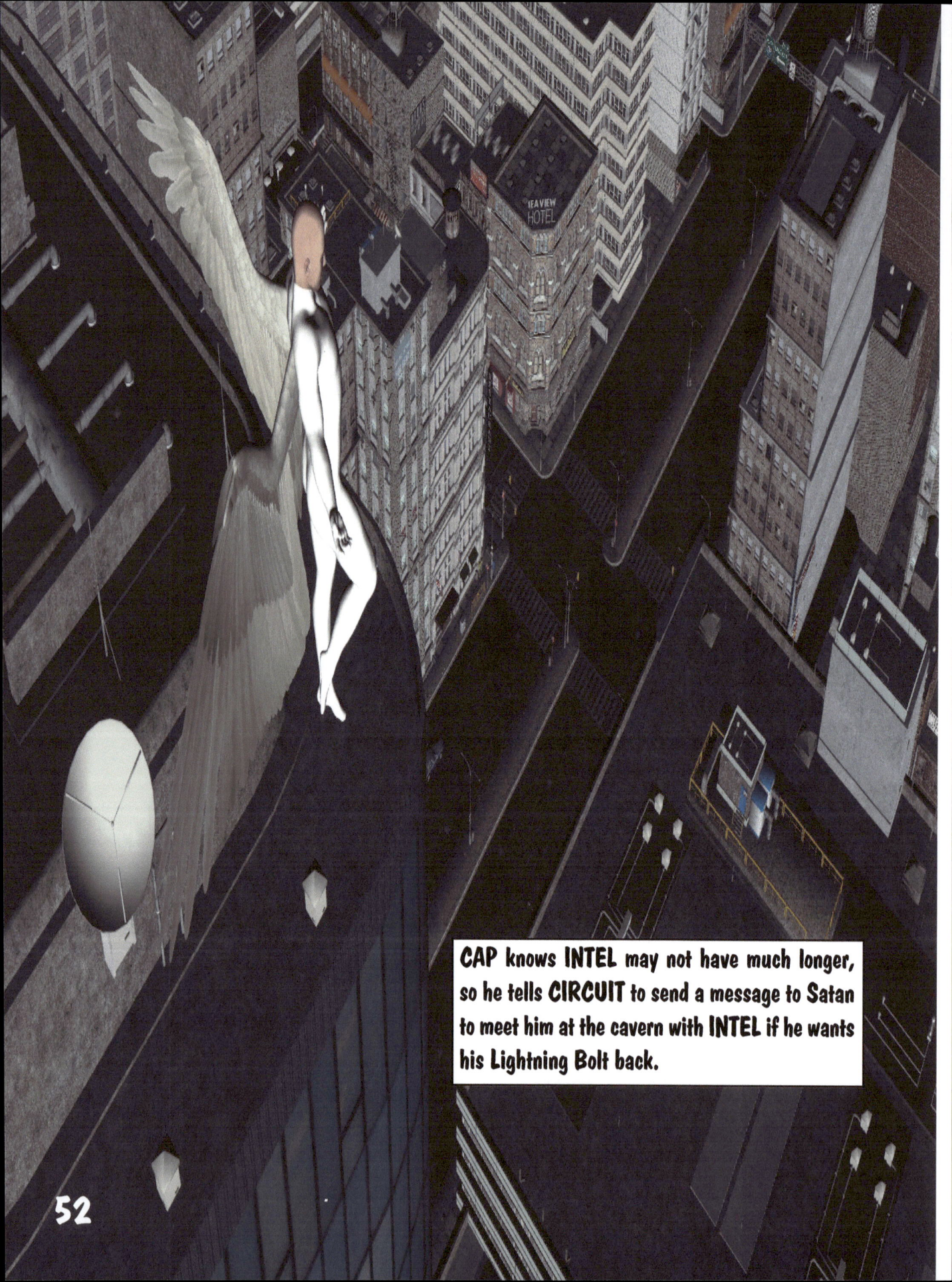

CAP knows **INTEL** may not have much longer, so he tells **CIRCUIT** to send a message to Satan to meet him at the cavern with **INTEL** if he wants his Lightning Bolt back.

BACK at OPS...

GENERAL DARKWING gives **CAP** the Key and shows him the location of Lightning Bolt.

CAP tells him his plan is not to give it back to Satan, just make him believe he will.

At the Cavern, which is ground zero for Satan and his demons...

CAP demands Satan release INTEL...

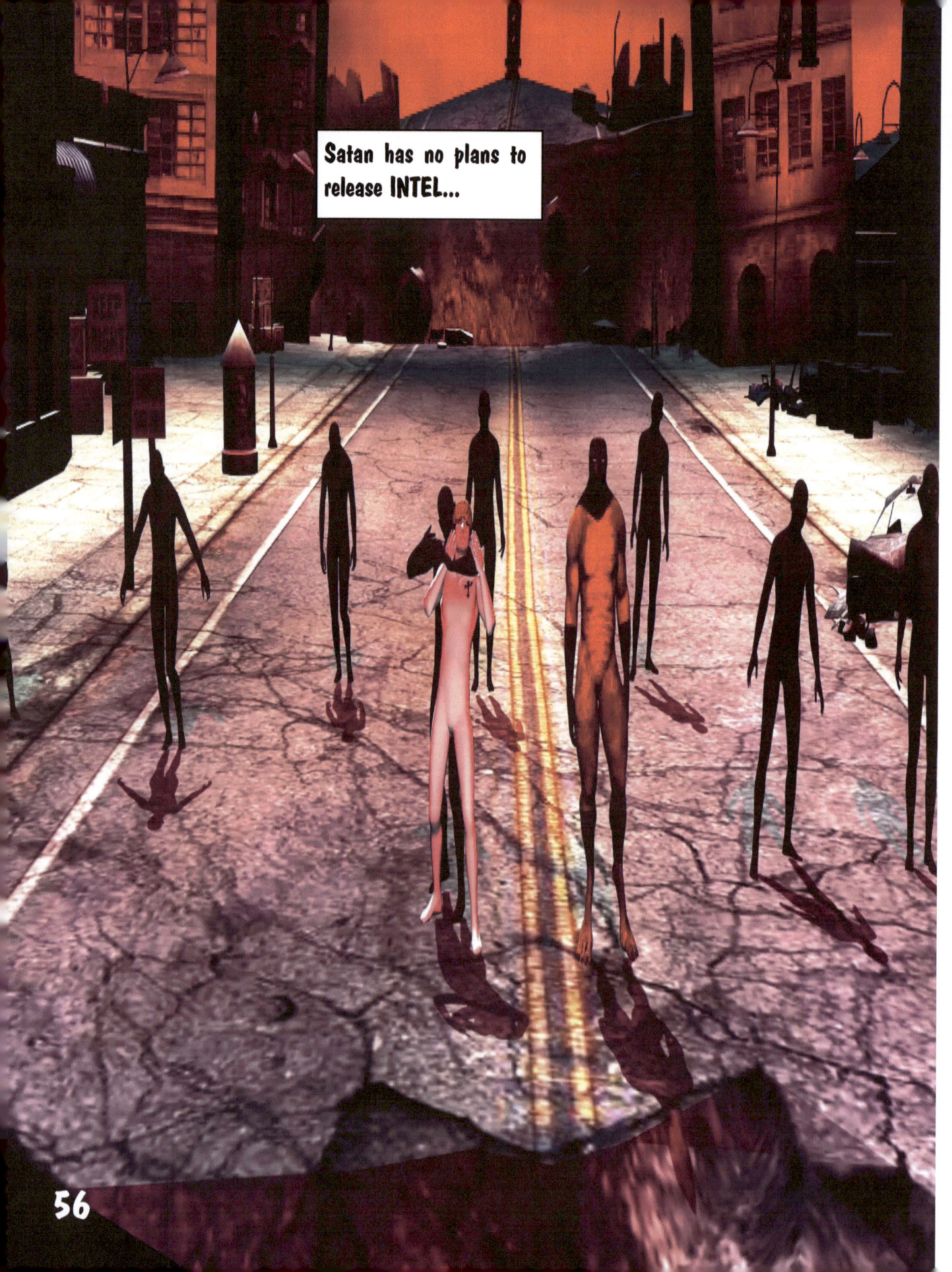

Satan has no plans to release INTEL...

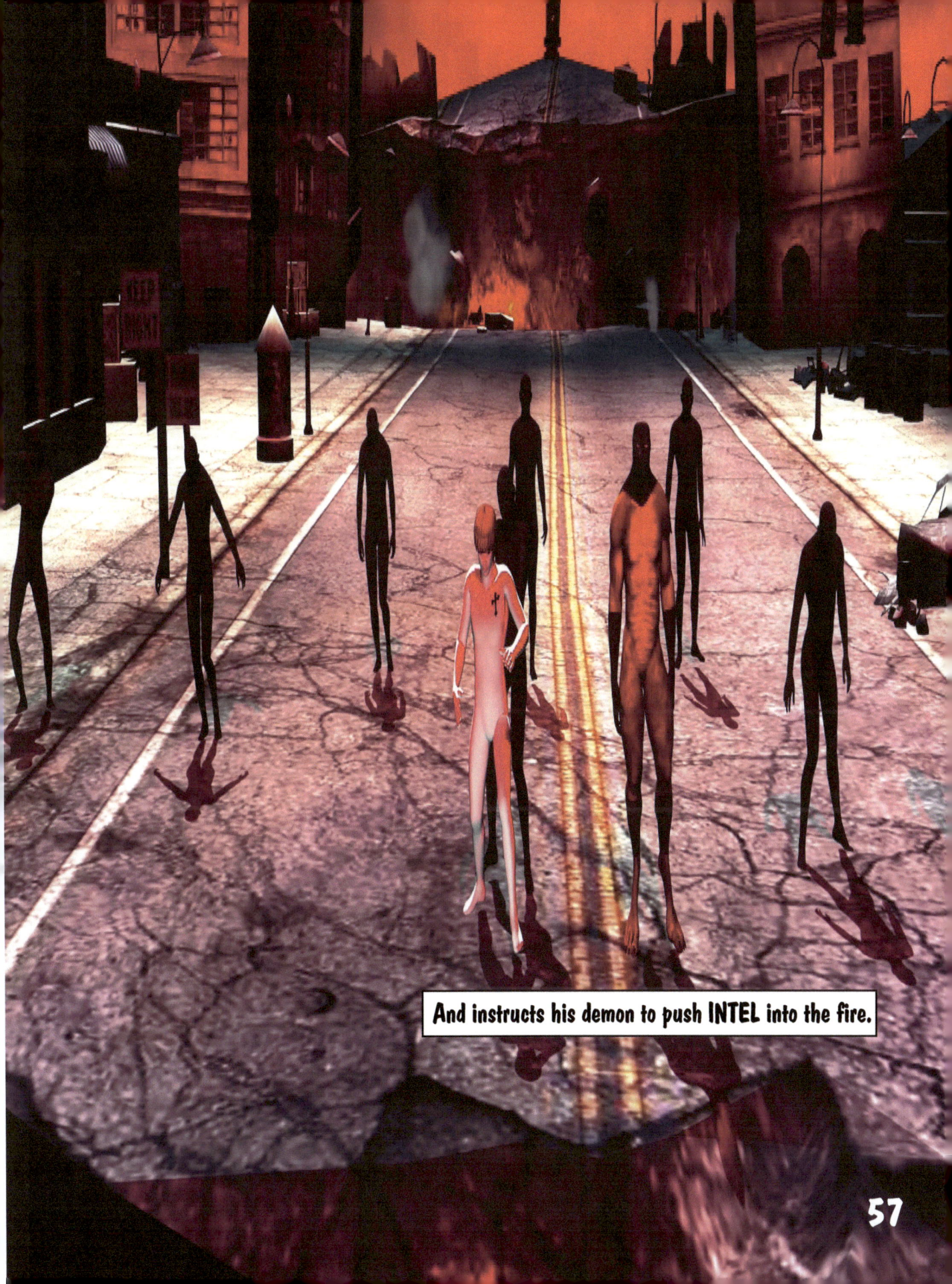

And instructs his demon to push **INTEL** into the fire.

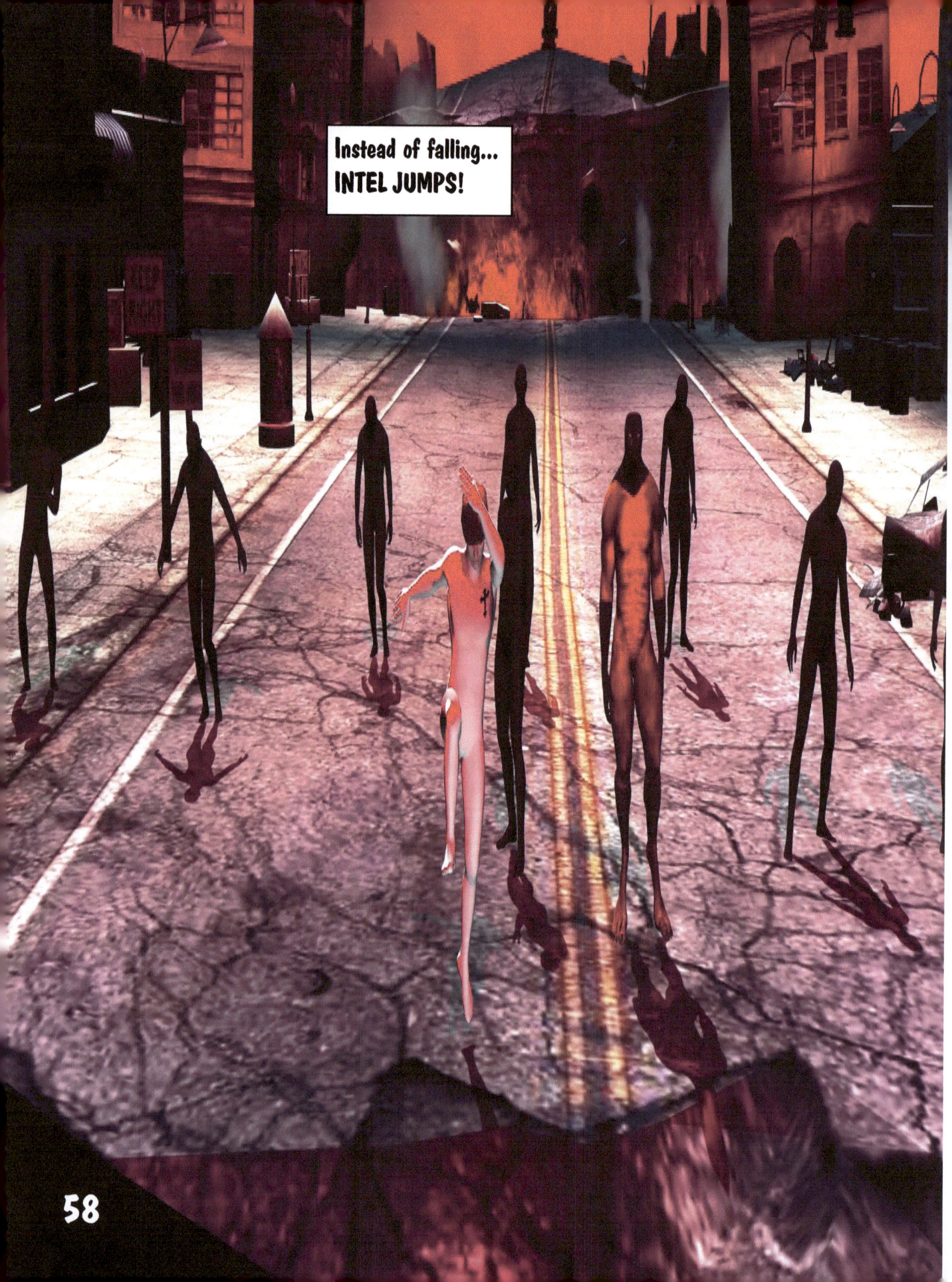

Instead of falling...
INTEL JUMPS!

FOX couldn't help her teammate when he was captured, but this time...

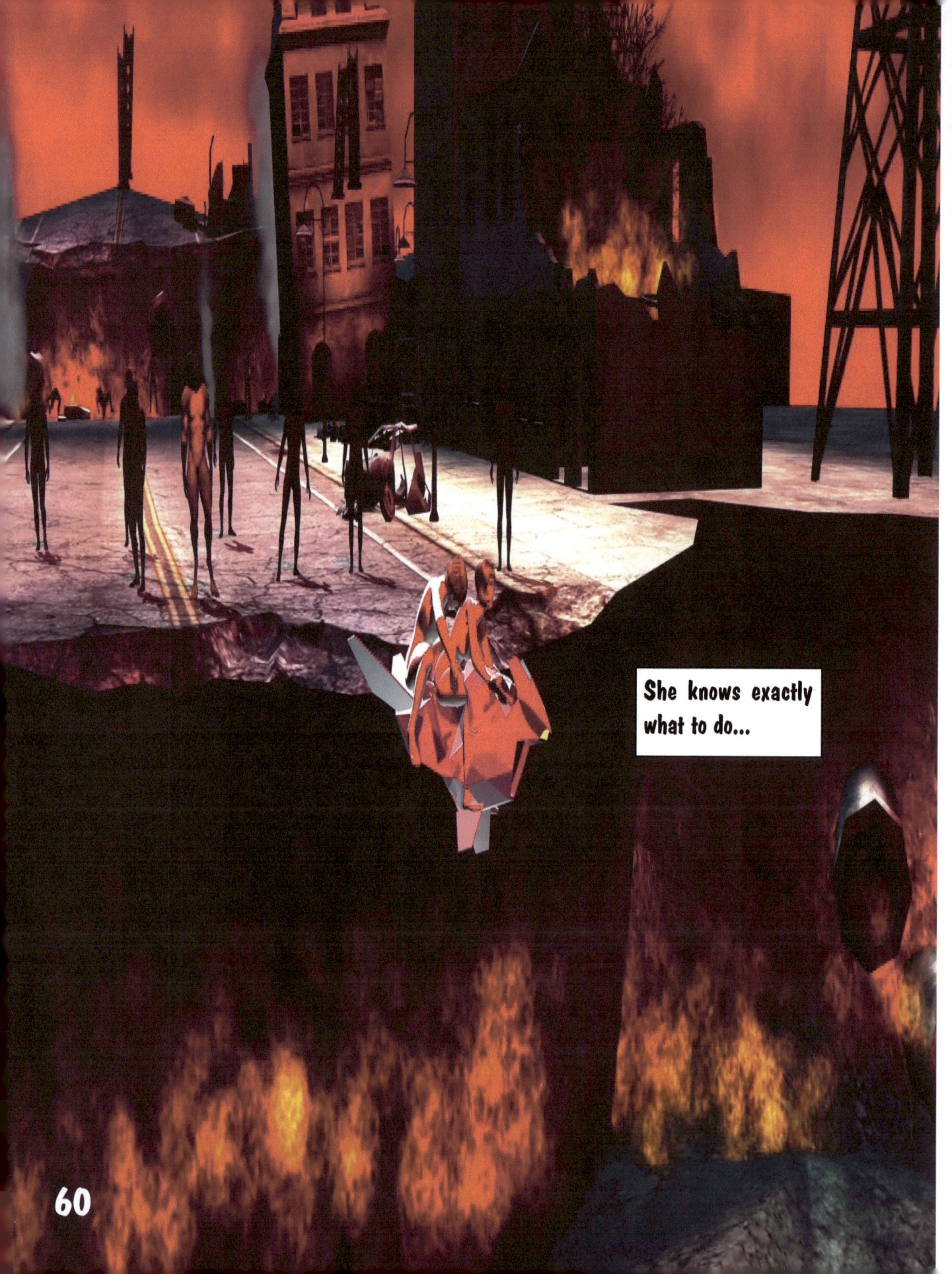

She knows exactly what to do...

...to help ensure his safe return.

Satan knows this is not a battle he can win today... so he turns and walks away.

As he is leaving he tells CAP that the battle has only just begun.

STRENGTH gets angry at the demon that was holding INTEL so he picks him up...

...and SLAMS him to the ground!

65

Many other team members come out from hiding behind a barrier...
but CAP tells everyone to stand down. This battle has to be won on different ground.

Will CAP use Lightning Bolt against Satan? Get this answer and more in Book 4 of Demons in the Darkness.

And see videos clips from this book and the animated trailer for the upcoming film at... PastorKeith.org/trailer.

www.ingramcontent.com/pod-product-compliance
Lightning Source LLC
Chambersburg PA
CBHW041426090426
42741CB00002B/45